Love Is

CRAIG R DURRANT

BALBOA.PRESS
A DIVISION OF HAY HOUSE

Balboa Press books may be ordered through booksellers or by contacting:

Balboa Press
A Division of Hay House
1663 Liberty Drive
Bloomington, IN 47403
www.balboapress.com
1 (877) 407-4847

Print information available on the last page.

ISBN: 978-1-9822-3365-5 (sc)
ISBN: 978-1-9822-3367-9 (hc)
ISBN: 978-1-9822-3366-2 (e)

Library of Congress Control Number: 2019918080

Balboa Press rev. date: 11/06/2019

To C. D., the angel who inspired me to know

CAUTION: PLEASE READ THIS

CONTENTS

Introduction xi

Section 1: ?

Chapter 1 Love Isn't Sex 1
Chapter 2 The Analogy 5
Chapter 3 The Raindrop 11
Chapter 4 Unconditional 17

Section 2: Love Is ...

Chapter 5 Love Is Naked 27
Chapter 6 Is Love Clothed? 37
Chapter 7 Love Is Free 43

Section 3: One

Chapter 8 Love Is Surrender 59
Chapter 9 One 75
Chapter 10 Love Is Sex 83

INTRODUCTION

WHAT IS LOVE? I THOUGHT I knew—until I was asked. With the realization that I didn't know what it is, I decided to learn. I was asking a wonderful lady who I cared for to trust me and to follow me into the unknown, and as a leader, I was supposed to do whatever it took to know. This book was written for her, and I have chosen to leave the wording personal like I would in a letter, text, or e-mail. I know there are things she has experienced, and I know that understanding is already in place. Only my personal experiences are brought out; her life and privacy are kept private.

Life taught me what love isn't—or I recognized many things that I initially thought were love before I realized they were just imitations of the real thing. As I learned what it isn't, I began to understand what it is. I also began to remember and believe in what I want in this area of my life.

This led to knowing that *I already have everything I need in order to be happy,* along with some other things that have changed my life in positive ways.

Some questions may be answered later. Maybe you have your own answers for some of them.

Every chapter is tied together and interrelated. They build on each other and may seem like overviews of what has already been covered. My intent is that different aspects will come out when things are written about in a different light. Every topic is of equal value, but at the same time, some are more important depending on where we are in life.

This book is meant to be part of the understanding. In other words, there is more to love than any of us can accurately describe to everyone in one hundred pages or more. It is progressive, and in ten years, our views will have shifted along with our waistlines and hair colors.

Enjoy, laugh, and smile.
Craig

SECTION I

?

CHAPTER 1

Love Isn't Sex

WHAT? ARE YOU SURE? LOOK at Hollywood and all the romance novels. They sure make sex look like love. I used to believe that sex meant love and love meant sex—and then the divorce came, and I, the typical male, learned that I didn't know what love is. Now, I can pretend to know what women think. That is a favorite pastime of some of the male species. They give themselves names like *man, doctor, boyfriend, husband,* and a variety of other self-important titles. But in truth, I don't. And because I am human, I know a little about love. I offer some guidance and direction. Love, as it develops, gives us the ability to connect with each other in such a way that we can know what the other is thinking.

For many years, the intimate bedroom scenes—the sex and the orgasms of life—appeared to be the crowning moments, the ultimate experience, heaven on earth, and more, and it can be when it is combined with love. If the act of sex were love, then the sick and repulsive acts of incest and rape and forced sex in marriage would be acts of love.

Consensual casual sex is more acceptable in society. Two people come together just for the pleasure, the companionship, or whatever else they want without the commitment that is an essential part of love. In these examples, the love is missing from the act. However, when love is the motivation and the essence of the sex is pure, it can be better than life, the next breath of air, or winning the lottery. Well, almost better than winning the lottery.

Throughout much of history, the male-female relationship was based on lust and control. Even the hippie movement during the 1960s, continuing to today, views love as sex and lust except without the control. That is why it is called *free*. It means there are no commitments or manipulating mandates. Women (and children) were treated as objects, and the prevailing attitude was women were possessions to be bought and sold. Sadly, this controlling attitude is alive and dominates the lives of most men who look at women as sex objects for pleasure—without respect or commitment. This has resulted in women using sex to manipulate and control men by placing requirements, like asking for money or favors, for the privileges of companionship and sex. We both know that this is a guaranteed way to drive the man crazy.

Going to the Bible, especially the Old Testament, or other

ancient writings is mostly useless. Most of the references are about how the woman was viewed by the man instead of how to be one with the woman in every way, including sex. Many movies and books portray women—and sometimes men—as sex slaves, objects of lust, and possessions to control. They either grant life or take it away based on the ability to please and make the men happy. If they wanted or desired real love, then the truth that it is to be found within ourselves was often beyond their understanding. We live in an amazing society where we have choices and laws that pretend to give everyone equal rights with no conditions as to gender, nationality, or skin color. Yet in many so-called relationships, the woman remains a servant-sex slave-nanny-living companion who is also expected to work outside the home to help provide for the family.

The good news is that some men are beginning to stand up and be *men* instead assholes and jerks. Men are beginning to treat women as equals in every role, especially at home with the kids and in the bedroom. Many are learning to lead by example and say, "Come. Follow me." instead of "Do as I say" with a my-way-or-the-highway attitude. Women are learning to be women instead of nags and bitches. They are learning to build their men with compliments instead of withholding themselves and nagging and trash-talking about their men. Both men and women are learning how to give of themselves in ways that only a few have mastered—and that we worship in movies and daydreams.

Then we learn that through sex and other areas of intimacy, we are giving of ourselves in progressive ways that are the ultimate in creation. As we love our companions with our total and complete hearts, bodies, and souls, we naturally include the types of sex that we enjoy as a couple. Love includes sex, but it is not limited to sex. Sex may or may not include love; therefore, love isn't sex. Love is more than any physical act or touch. It is the power in all of life.

I also learned that love doesn't include force, dominance, being the dictator (masculine) or the bitch (feminine), being a wimp, having a better-than-you attitude, anger, hurt feelings, lying (especially during intimacy), secrets, being needy, and much, much more.

It could take pages to discuss all the things that love isn't and reinforce the hurt feelings and broken promises, but I like to keep my blood pressure in the good and healthy range. Instead, let us focus more on what it is and how we get back into the flowing stream of ecstasy and bliss and become a permanent part of it. I like to feel good at my very core—in the center of my soul—and I want you to feel this goodness, which is beyond pleasure. I hope you come and experience it with me in the pages that follow.

CHAPTER 2

The Analogy

WHAT IS IT LIKE TO be one with the song, the ocean breeze, the mountain air, the incoming tide, or the flowing stream? What is it like to be one with the raindrop as it falls gently on our faces and then trickles down to fall and become part of all creation? What is it like to be one with the energy of life—the things we may call good or bad or the pleasant and the unpleasant—and be able to just be and experience them for what they are without judgments?

My favorite thing to do—besides be with the one I have chosen to love—is to be in nature and listen to its song. Occasionally, I'm able to get out of my head and my emotions just long enough to be present in the moment and become one with and connect with the greatness that is surrounding me. It is beautiful and seems to include all, even in the simplest settings.

The bird sings because it has a song to sing. It isn't out to change the world. It is sharing the song that it has within its heart, and we have the choice to let it annoy us or bless our lives with its simplistic beauty. You and I cannot force the bird to sing. It is impossible to force another to be one with the song. It is a choice, an individual choice. It is love.

As I become one with the music, the stream, the breeze, or the raindrop rolling down my skin, I relax into it and feel with my heart and more. I feel with more than just my heart. I feel with my whole body and soul. At the same time, I let go of my desire to be in control and free. I surrender to the essence of the all-creative power in that tiny drop of rain and the unseen sound of the music of life. I choose to give it love and to receive love from it. All judgments stop. In other words, I let it just be and acknowledge all that is happening in the moment. I'm not defining it with things such as liking or disliking it, good or bad, or right or wrong. I do notice everything, including warm and cold, soft and hard, fast and slow, and how it all becomes good. All resistance has ended. There is no opposition. It never opposed me and never will. It was only I who resisted and was scared to surrender to the music.

I wanted to be free to have my own identity, and in my ignorance and childishness, I tried to force my fake *oneness* of expectations and conditionality onto my surroundings. It didn't work; it kept me from becoming one with them. I didn't realize that they—the raindrop, the bird, the sunset, and the sunrise—are already one. It was me who was out of harmony with all of them. I didn't realize that I was out of harmony with love. It is in and through this surrender of my natural will and resistance to their song that I felt freedom. How can I explain something that can only be experienced? How can I express how I feel like the whole world is perfect when everything is the same except for my attitude in this moment? Maybe I will learn how to do it someday. A beautiful lady asked me what love is, and I began to know because she asked.

In this act of becoming one with the music, I feel as if it is breathing me. Even the raindrop takes over and carries me and breathes for me, and gravity has no pull. It is like I am floating in the ocean. All my needs are taken care of.

As the music moves me, I experience oneness, freedom, security, life, resilience, and completion. I become the wineglass that is complete and empty at the same time, and then I am filled with the wine of the oneness of the present moment. It is gentle and seductive. It is exhilarating and calming. It is all I ever wanted. It is complete in all its simplicity and its intricate design. It tells me that this is what completes everything in life, that this oneness is the essence of joy and what I call the feeling of love.

I feel like I am at home with my source of life. Thinking comes from a source that is different than the mind. Thoughts come from my heart and my body. They are pure and innocent. They inspire me and lift me and take me places that I never knew existed. They expand my view and understanding. I am filled with emotions like compassion, kindness, allowing, inclusion, forgiveness, acceptance, peace, gratitude, love, calmness, and being present. There is no need or desire to leave the present for anything in the past or in the future. In fact, they are distractions and lower energies.

Any thought or attempt to understand, to define or choose a favorite part, is abandoned. Each and every piece, color, and hue is equal in its beauty and oneness. It would be like asking me what my favorite color of the rainbow is. I answer, "All of them. If one was missing, there would be no rainbow. I like them all." Any attempt to figure it out takes us out of the moment of oneness. It is as if we surrender the mind to the flow of energy and go with it. There is no thinking—just awareness.

These, depending on the moment, can be erotic and sensual, rejuvenating and inspiring, or all of them combined. For me, they are always healing. Things that used to be overwhelming are now funny, and I laugh at myself for being too serious or too much in my ego mind.

There is no neediness or wimpiness or weakness. They are replaced with confidence and true power. In this moment of being present, all expectations and conditions are abandoned. The only condition is to follow the inner voice or calling that inspires me to be one with the moment. I give love as I gift all that I am to the Source of Life, and in return, I receive all that Source is gifting to me.

I realize I already have everything I need in order to be happy, and now I am able to share it with the raindrop, the bird, and all that is in my presence. I desire to share it with others, to share it with you, as an individual who is inseparably connected with all of life, and the understanding comes that I can guide and inspire with love and gentleness. This gift can never be forced on another or on myself.

The understanding tells me that becoming one with my lover, my companion, my wife is better than being one with all of nature. That when the masculine and feminine come together in divine unison—with sex being the ultimate act of oneness in both gifting and receiving—the joy is much greater than what I experience with nature, music, or dance.

We can like the music and hear it and choose not to be one with it. We can choose to be one with it and not be able to feel the love in that moment because of earlier choices. However, that does not mean that we can't or don't have the ability to love or harmonize with them. We have the ability, and it can take years of gentle self-love to transform us into who we really are: one with each other, the raindrop, the song of the bird, and all of creation.

There is hope in every ray of sunlight and in every smile on the face of the moon. As we look for it, we will find it. Let us fill our cups and share them with others.

CHAPTER 3

The Raindrop

IF YOU PRAY FOR RAIN, are you prepared to deal with the mud? How many raindrops does it take before we call it rain?

There isn't anything special about a single drop of rain—or is there? It has no will of its own, and yet each one accomplishes its purpose. It is perfect as it is. The rain may fall as tiny droplets or as drenching streams. It may become hail or a soft, velvety snowflake, depending on the environment. It is beauty in every drop; there is no ugliness in it.

In *The Hidden Messages in Water,* Masaru Emoto shows us that every drop has a memory—and that it becomes one with us, our thoughts, and our emotions. And then it shares that memory with everything. It is part of its nature and perfection to do this. It can be several feet away from us and still become one with us. It is living.

It doesn't matter if we are rich or poor, happy or sad, sick or healthy, religious or not, or any other this or that. To the perfect drop of rain, we are all the same. We are perfect as we are and have unlimited potential. The raindrop comes from the highest places and flows to the lowest of the lows in the darkest hours. It can clean the air and let the sun shine on us in its brightest hours. It is part of the essence of life. When we are born, more than 90 percent of our bodies is made of these perfect little drops of rain. We are more like the raindrop than any other thing.

It gives to us no matter what—even when we try to divert it with the umbrella or rain slicker. We can choose to isolate ourselves from water. We can choose to say we don't need it, but that is a lie. If we take the water out of us, then the result is obvious: we become dried-up old prunes and dirty old men.

This little drop nourishes all the food we eat. It is part of everything we drink. It gives us life. We use it to wash and clean our bodies, our clothes, and our dishes. We use it to remove odors and to make things fresh and like new again. We use it to recycle and create everything we use in life—from plastic to clothes to paper to glass.

This little drop removes the poisons from our bodies and replaces them with life. Unlike alcohol and drugs, which remove this life from our bodies and leave toxins in their place, it is meant to flow. Its purpose is to share. If it pools too long and becomes stagnant, it becomes toxic to all life. Even the oceans flow, and in this flowing, there is life.

Love isn't stagnant!

Love is flowing!

Love is a raindrop!

How many drops of love does it take before we call it love? Is it a weekend shower of erotic emotions and sensuality? Is it a one-time feeling that they are perfect for me? Maybe it is going through a period of time to see if this is just a season of love? Does this take a month, six months, a year, or more? Can we handle the mud in the rain and the dust in the dry times? Is it possible to preserve love and share it in the dry times like we do with water in reservoirs? I think we all have pools of love within us. Some are open and close to the surface; others are hidden and require great searching within in order to find because of how deep they are. These deep ones are the sweetest, the most difficult to develop, and they may last for all time or more. They are to be understood with experience and are beyond description.

Love is a choice—or is it?

Love is a raindrop, and it flows. It is in everything that nourishes life. It is everything that adds value to our lives. It is the building block of existence. Love is our essence.

In my craziness, I have watched the raindrop land on my skin and soak into my body as it rolls across my arm. I have imagined being one with it, giving it love, and receiving love in return. As a kid, I would run out of the house to be out in the rain and splash in the puddles and let the rain showers breathe me and carry me away. I was one with them in the moment. Thinking of these times brings joy and happiness to my heart, and my mouth becomes speechless because my heart is now the speaker. I am healed, for a moment, and the world is perfect. I am inspired. I am in love. I feel as if I could fly. I feel like gravity is just a myth that was made up to keep me here, to keep me from being all that I could be, but I need it to teach me how to fly and be all that I can be.

The rain has been my tear of love and broken hearts. It has nourished me and healed me as I became one with it and felt its perfect loving oneness.

There have been seasons in which I resisted and placed myself in the lowest and darkest nights and cursed the rain because I was weak and not the rain. These were seasons of anguish and fear. They came from the ego and not the heart or soul. They came from choosing not to love in certain ways, withholding love, or becoming stagnant. During these seasons of resistance, the raindrop, in its loving wisdom, brought inner storms that cracked and destroyed the dams and walls that were making me stagnant and toxic to life and to myself. The inner voice that emanates love guided me to return to my source, to the part of me that is one with the music and the tiny drop of rain. I was guided to step out of the comfort zone of the ego and become one with the flow of love.

It would be great to take your hand and be one in the

rain, to feel it together, in the moment. Time would stop as we exist as one with creation as the rain falls in perfection and becomes one with our bodies and souls. Worries and fears cease to exist; they are foreign and repulsive. This is love; we are one with God and nature and with each other.

May each tiny raindrop wash away our tears with the love and perfection of being one with us.

CHAPTER 4

Unconditional

I HAD A DREAM, A romantic dream, that I would love my wife, whoever she is, unconditionally. At the time, I had no idea what unconditional love meant, how to do it, or what it required, but it sounded good, and it is what I wanted. In the romanticism, I had many wonderful ideas and dreams; some I continue to believe in, but many were not unconditional, and I let them go. Earlier, before I wrote this, I realized that every condition that I place on love is about me needing another person to be a certain way in order for me to give them my love and for me to be happy. I realized that these conditions have nothing to do with you or with them. They don't determine whether you are a good person or a bad person; they don't determine whether you are deserving or not deserving. All they are able to determine is whether or not my love is conditional or unconditional. If I have a requirement for you to do, be, or act a certain way, then it is conditional.

Maybe I want love with just a few conditions. Who is to say that this is right or wrong? What if my wife, whoever she may be, decided to change her lifestyle after we were married and became a bisexual whore who stripped in the living room for other men or women to earn a little extra spending money for drugs? Or what if she became ultrareligious and took a vow of celibacy for the rest of her life? These are conditions that movies and books are made of.

There are others that are closer to home and to the heart of everyday life: spending the vacation money on something else, changing plans in the middle of a project and not letting us know, or making decisions that affect us without our consent. There are many more, and we know what they are; talking about them makes them bigger. In my heart, I believe that if I can't unconditionally love the one I am with, then it is lacking in its authentic pureness and depth.

In my experience, the closer I get and the more I commit to you or anyone else, the more conditional I want to make my love. I think this is part of being human. The closer I get to you, the more I open and reveal my heart. I feel naked and vulnerable—exposed to you—as I do this. At the same time, I also feel that the love is deep and good, real and genuine. However, the child in me wants to make conditions or promises to do or not do certain things that go beyond respect. These may come from fear or from a my-way-or-the-highway attitude. It is definitely not love.

There is one condition that is part of any and every happy and meaningful intimate relationship: being committed to that inner voice, which is called *intuition* or *inspiration*. If and when the voice tells us to give our love unconditionally, then we are to give it—for our benefit and for their benefit. If the voice tells us to get out of the relationship, then get out. If it tells us to let them go, then let them go. We might be asked to let them go and continue to give them unconditional love. If so, then it is in our best interests—and their best interests. This could mean letting go of our attachment to them to be a certain way, to make us happy, to desire specific outcomes, or giving love no matter what. This is still one of my ideals and remains a work in progress. It is continual. As long as we are alive, these things are in a constant state of change.

In the different types of relationships—parent-child, friends, casual acquaintance, strangers, boyfriend-girlfriend, committed lovers, husband-wife—we have different expectations and conditions. For me, the closest relationship is committed lovers who are husband and wife. I can easily give unconditional stranger love or parent-child or child-parent love. In the other types, conditional things that I never knew existed begin to come out. It took a committed lover relationship to expose them. It often takes being together in the ugly and the beautiful—the light and the dark times—to bring them out. This is good, especially when we are looking to be our better selves.

It takes going through the *conditions* to know that I can—and we can—love unconditionally. It is easy to say, "I can do that" or "If they had done it this way or not done it that way, then it would have worked." We don't know the behind-the-scenes or closed-door events. We don't know the thoughts and broken expectations and promises they have had.

Unconditional forgiveness and acceptance require courage and strength. The emotionally and mentally weak cannot do it, yet they are the ones who are the most demanding that others do it! In doing this, they are rigid, demanding, and forceful. They dictate their wills on us because they *know* best—or so they say. Those who are powerful enough to do it know that it is much more difficult and challenging to actually live it. Therefore, they are gentle, kind, and compassionate as they encourage, inspire, and guide us to become love. And then, with personal example, they lead the way and show us how it is done.

There is no right way or wrong way in all of this. If you or anyone else wants conditional love in your life, then that is good. If they want *unconditional love,* which is now a condition, then they must choose someone who can give it or desire it and work toward being it. By the nature of evolving, most of us have a long way to go before the ideal is reached. If we want to give unconditionally, we must be ready to give it every time—unless the inner voice tells us not to.

Unconditional love is part of becoming one with each other and with the music and the raindrop. Try becoming one with the music and nature and having requirements that they be a certain way, act a certain way, or do exactly what we ask them to. It doesn't work! How can we feel free when we don't allow them to be free?

Unconditional love is unconditional freedom for us, for ourselves, and for them. We are allowing them to grow and be all they can be as we give them what only we can give them: the piece of our essence that we call love. Anybody can give money, food, or the physical amenities. Only I can give my love and commitment, and only you can give the love that comes from you. That love is you.

When the husband and the wife come together at the same time with unconditional love, they are able to become one with each other. With the music, ecstasy takes on a new meaning. I have sensed it; it's like watching an amazing trailer for a movie and then attempting to describe the movie. I want to see the movie.

When I got married, I took a vow of "in sickness and health." I vowed to be there no matter what—even if she burned the toast, made me mad, or acted like a you-know-what. I dislike prenuptial agreements because they say, "Hey,

I don't trust you—and here are some of my conditions." However, if the prenup was more of a plan for different gradations of how to become one in our finances and all of life over a period of five or ten years, then it could possibly have a place.

Before we can gift unconditional love to another, we need to be able to gift it to ourselves and receive that gift with an open heart. The same can be said for every quality and object. In order to trust another, we must trust ourselves first.

In order to truly give a gift, we must be willing to receive it from others and ourselves. If we can't do this, then it is coming from a place self-deprivation or self-righteousness, which is an attitude of *less than* or *better than another*. In this condition, we are rejecting the fact that we come from the same source and that we are equal, and at the same time, we are unique. It is like how all the colors of the rainbow are equal since they all come from the same source—light—and are unique in all their different colors and hues. If we were to take out one of the colors or part of one of the colors, then it would be incomplete. The perfection and oneness would become distorted—just like how our attitudes can distort and resist the source of our unconditional love.

When we strive to align and harmonize our attitudes with being one with our Source, then all of the colors are included with all of their hues and differences. We shine in our unique beauty and perfection. In this completeness, we can be the glass or the wine—the glass to receive or the wine to give—and we can do it in completeness together, in the pleasant and the unpleasant.

With a daily dose of a little love and commitment, we change the world, just like the song of the bird changes the world.

SECTION II

Love Is ...

CHAPTER 5

Love Is Naked

LOVE IS NAKED IN EVERY way, and it has nothing to hide. Like the naked dreams, we are exposed and vulnerable, and everyone can see all of our insecurities, imperfections, and shortcomings. However, they see them as strengths because they are clothed in love. It is naked in the sense that there is nothing between you and me, in a figurative way of speaking, skin to skin and flesh to flesh.

In intimacy, our *clothes* can represent words and actions that are used to cover our insecurities, fears, shortcomings, doubts, and the ego's neediness. As we take off the clothes or stories that we use to cover the inner self, we often feel self-conscious, exposed, and vulnerable. At the same time, love is free; it is free of all the clothes and stories. Being emotionally naked is free to be authentic and genuine; we could call it "in the flesh."

One of the mottos I live by—be your authentic self— is part of the reason I am open as I express myself in transparency that seems naked with you. It reveals who I am in open honesty, and if I were to lie, it would stand out like a white boy in Motown.

Being naked takes guts. It is trusting in the unseen. Every self-conscious thought eventually becomes exposed; nothing is hidden. At first, I think, *This is really, really bad,* but as I relax into the best feelings of the moment, I am able to feel goodness.

One of the scariest things I have ever done is becoming naked or open with others. This isn't for the weak of heart or those who live from their ego instincts. Becoming naked or open with our dreams, feelings, emotions, and thoughts is difficult at first, but then it becomes very rewarding. It makes us free to say all the things we wanted to say but were too scared or bashful or private to say them. It would be much easier to take off my clothes and be in my birthday suit than to be emotionally naked, and it is different than those who tell the world everything with no respect for privacy. It is about two people revealing themselves to each other and keeping all of their desires and dreams in their hearts. It is about respect and trust; it is revealing who I am to you in every way.

In becoming one with the song of the bird and the breeze as it moves the trees and the grass, I open myself to them as we become one. In moving with the breeze as it carries the song, they move me and breathe for me. All of the secrets and desires that lay hidden in my heart and mind are shared with them. There is no laughing or mocking them; there is only respect and acknowledgement. Some thoughts feel better or more pleasing than others, and others seem to disappear. There is no judgment; there is allowing and flow. New ideas can lead to deeper intimacy in the bedroom. Some ideas can lead to new directions in life. It is the same when two people come together; it doesn't matter if it is two others or my companion and me.

Touch—skin-to-skin contact—is essential. It could be as simple as touching your arm, a kiss, or total intimacy. With touch, there can be a flow of energy or power. An event recorded in the New Testament helps illustrate this.

In a crowd of people, Christ stopped and asked, "Who touched me?"

His disciples, puzzled at this, said something like, "What do you mean? We are in a crowd, and people are constantly bumping and touching us."

He said that He felt power or virtue flowing out of Him to another; this flow is part of love. Many people are sensitive to this touch and can feel this flow of energy. It can be felt between animals and us. It can be felt between plants and us. It can be felt between people, and when it is, it heals and energizes both of them. Having felt this flow of energy and power between all of these, I want more of it, and that requires me to be naked in every way—mentally, emotionally, and in all of my desires to be one—with no hidden agendas or intentions.

Love is open.

Love is honest.

When we are naked, the only option is to trust. In the act of being naked, we are naturally honest. There are times when we are sorting out and discovering *us*. In these times, it may seem like we are changing things around. There are times of chaos and confusion, and times we just don't know. It is hard for the ego—if not impossible—for it to say that it doesn't know. During these times, it is very important to be open, to be completely open, and ask, "I know that you don't know, but if you did know, what would it be?" This is asked in kindness with compassion and a gentle heart.

When I first began this with myself, there was so much resistance. I resisted it. There were parts of me—thoughts and desires—that I wanted to keep hidden from everyone, including myself. I despised myself, and it felt like a lie to even think that I loved me. How can I give love to another if I can't give it to myself? I knew it was essential to love ourselves before we could truly love another. I began the mirror exercise. I don't know who created it or where I first read about it, but it changed my life.

During the mirror exercise, we look into a mirror, and as we look into our eyes, we sincerely tell us, the one in the mirror, that we love them. We call them (our reflection) by name and say, "I love you." We also thank them for a few specific things that we like about them.

The first time I attempted to do this, I made it three days in a row. However, I never completed it because it felt like such a major lie. My stomach became so sick that I was ready to retch and vomit. My face turned pale, and my hands and legs became cold and began to shake and quiver. My body began to sweat, and I felt cold all over. All sorts of psychosomatic symptoms began to come out as I attempted to tell myself in the mirror—with sincerity—that I love you. I stopped doing the exercise, and over the next year or so, I worked on being more compassionate and appreciative of me—and then I did the exercise again.

A year later, it still felt like a lie to say, "I love you, Craig." However, I could finally feel gratitude for the other things I said. Then after a couple of weeks of doing this, I began to feel self-love. It was sincere and genuine. I now do it almost every day as I get out of the shower, shave, and brush my teeth. I have discovered that the more authentic love I give myself, the more I can give to my kids, to you, and to others. I call this a miracle.

This exercise exposed me to me, and I became naked. I wanted to hide at first, but there wasn't any place deep enough or dark enough to hide in. I wanted to hide from myself, from God, and from the entire world, including the music and the songs of nature and all that I had once felt oneness with. It was impossible to hide from it, but I knew that not even death could accomplish this.

The miracle took place in the journey. As I gave love to myself with a naked heart and soul, I learned that love isn't secrets and half-truths. I learned that it isn't force or disrespect. I learned that love is sincerely loving myself and appreciating all of the uniqueness that is me. It is being happy with all of my abilities and disabilities and all of my likes and dislikes and just being me. I had a distorted view of perfection, and it took a few years to replace it with acceptance and allowing and more.

Love is accepting.

Love is allowing.

How can I become one with the raindrop if I don't allow it to fall on me? How can I become one with it if I can't allow myself to accept it? How can I become one with it if I can't allow myself to choose to become one with it? True acceptance and allowing begins with accepting the self and then allowing the self to be. The self must be present, be real, and be naked or open and honest. The self must be able to desire and want things and be happy, which means following inspiration and our true Source.

In order to become one with the raindrop, it is essential that I allow it to be all that it is—no more and no less. I accept it as my equal, and arrogance—the notion of being better than or less than anyone or anything—is abandoned.

The sound of each drop as it falls and lands on this living world becomes music to my ears. It becomes music in my soul, and it becomes a part of my soul. Each drop adds to it and never takes anything away from it. It is only and always goodness. Power, without effort, flows, and this energy, which is beyond words, instantly and simultaneously permeates the body and flows out from the life source in every direction—up and down, left and right, forward and backward—in and out of us and to all that is and was and ever will be. To me, this is beautiful and erotic. It is creation and being a participant in and with the power that inspires and breathes all of life. This is ecstasy.

The spiral staircase allows us to go up or down and view the same scene. We see the center from every side and angle, and we see the outside world from many different angles. They are all different places in life and windows of beauty that we have choice to allow and accept. The more I allow myself to be myself, the more I am able to allow others to be themselves, and this helps me allow myself even more. The same is true with acceptance and every attribute of love. And with every step along the journey, everything we view takes on a slightly different hue or color.

If we resist this change, then we remove the self from the flow or the place of acceptance and allowing. A feeling of discontentment replaces the love we once felt. Only we can do the resisting. No one can do it for us or make us do it; it is our choice. Only we can cause the feelings of love or its absence within us as individuals. Love isn't resisting, joining any movement of resistance, or demanding that others be a certain way. Love is allowing and accepting. It is inclusive and flowing.

Love is flowing.

Love is inclusive.

Love isn't stagnant or separatist or segregated. Love flows like water and the raindrop; it touches the highest mountaintop and the coldest frozen situations and regions as gentle snowflakes. It flows in the smallest streams and the largest rivers. It comes from the highest of the highs and seeks the lowest of them all; it flows to the oceans and the seas of life. It is found in every living entity. Love, like water, includes everything and everyone.

If it were to exclude anything that is living, it would be excluding its very essence and would be resisting itself, which causes feelings of low self-worth and insufficiency. The ego or natural mind would try to compensate, increasing the destructive cycle of thoughts and beliefs of being better than another. That is resisting or opposing all the things we have in common. That resistance is the cause of the many words we use to describe different degrees or emotional states of love or the absence of love: despair, hate, envy, anger, pride, and so on.

Love isn't these low states of energy, but it flows to them, it includes them, it accepts them, and it nourishes them. Love is inclusive; like the raindrop, it is one with all of life. It can be as soft and gentle as a velvet snowflake or a warm summer mist. It can be as powerful and turbulent as a typhoon, a hurricane, or a tsunami that redefines the shape of our lives. Love is in all of these; resistance keeps us from seeing it and feeling it.

During the tsunamis and hurricanes of life, the essence of life is asking us to surrender to it. The ego hears *surrender* and thinks *death* and *loss* and *defeat*. Source is saying, "Surrender your attachments to the ego, and I will give you true life and the power to navigate and survive the storm."

As we let go of our resistance to the power and Source of life, we begin to feel the love of inspiration flowing and guiding us to ride the waves that had threatened to destroy us.

Love isn't needy or possessive; it includes and accepts and allows others to be those things. It nourishes them and invites them to be whole and to be free. It never withholds love from them; it may come in different forms or in ways the ego doesn't like or recognize. It may feel like it is going to destroy the very essence of our identity, expose us, and make us *naked* before God, the universe, and all of creation.

In arrogance, the ego claims to create love. It calls acts of force *tough love*. It renames *neediness* and *possessiveness* as *kindness* and *gentleness*. It calls addiction to attachment true love, and it gives others our power to be happy, authentic, and free, which leaves us feeling weak and controlled. It is sentimental, and it fails to see the light and the oneness of each changing moment. It resists surrendering to the present moment of becoming one with the song and being naked and open with each other; it has an agenda, which is called "survival at any cost."

Love is naked.

Love is as naked as a raindrop. We can see through it, but it is clothed with all of creation. In its open transparency, the raindrop can split light into all of its many colors and hues. Love, in its vulnerable authenticity, can transform the darkest, blackest, dirtiest lump of coal into the brightest, most sparkling diamond of life.

The raindrop asks, "Can you be one with me as I am one with you?" That is the same way the Source of love is asking if we can be one with love. Love is open, love is honest, love is accepting, and love is allowing. Love is flowing, and love is inclusive. It is transparent and has no hidden agenda or design. It is found in the thorns and deserts of life. It is found in the velvet rose and the light of the moon. It is softer than a snowflake or the kiss of your lips. It makes the touch of your lover's hand energize your soul, and it gives meaning to life. In its surrender, love is power.

Love is naked, and in this, it is clothed in and with authentic beauty.

CHAPTER 6

Is Love Clothed?

Is LOVE CLOTHED? WE USE clothes to keep us warm and to protect us from injuring our bodies. We use clothes to symbolize rank and segregation or to unify and show equality. We use them to accent our bodies and to look attractive, erotic, and seductive as well as to show respect and privacy. Love is clothed with qualities that accent its nakedness in all of its curves and muscles.

Love is clothed with integrity. It provides truth and honesty in the night; there are no lies to whisper here. It is clothed with a cloak of transparency that allows everyone, including ourselves, to see the real me. It is clothed with the stars of heaven and the flowers in the meadows. It bathes in the rivers and the streams; it blesses each and every drop as it touches the earth. It is clothed with beauty that can only be seen when we are clothed with love. We use metaphors to paint pictures of the indescribable and to clothe love in select ways so we can recognize and begin to understand it.

When it shows up wearing an unfamiliar outfit, we tend to label it as an imposter or a counterfeit. We find that what is kind and gentle to the life source may not be pleasant to the ego. Yet within this *unpleasantness,* we find fulfillment and completion in love.

Love is clothed with oneness in the inclusion of diversity, and that is much different than the symbolic oneness of wearing the same clothes for a spiritual endeavor or—even more drastic—the mandates of a governing body. It is almost impossible to be one in life if that oneness is mandated; in the mandate, life becomes a song with only one note that suppresses the life and flow of energy.

Love is clothed with the diversity of each note in the song of the bird, the tuning of the orchestra, and the sounds of the equipment working the roads and building the towns and cities we live in. It is clothed with the hearts of the people who serve without praise or reward. The sound of the siren is a melody of hope to those who are injured and to those who love them.

We write songs and poems to express and describe the feelings of love, and for many people, the closest they can get to it is the euphoria and ecstasy of sex. Many have spent their lives in the delusion of trying to create artificial methods to achieve all that love—only to be met with disappointment and addictions that have scarred the hearts and minds of millions.

We use words like *gentle, kind, infinite,* and *eternal* or *forgiveness, understanding,* and *integrity,* but those words limit the limitless essence of love. We clothe it with humor and respect but continue to fall short of all its beauty. To admire and appreciate it in its simplest form to its most intrinsic and complex creation that we call human life is insufficient in our description of love. And then we resort to saying love *isn't* because that seems to be easier to understand.

In the process of saying love is, we strip it and remove all the undesirable clothes or characteristics we have placed on it. We replace them with transparent metaphors of what love truly is in an attempt to leave it naked in its own power. I think it is impossible to fully and completely comprehend and understand love as living life in the bodies we have. As we progress in our understanding, our bodies are changed to make this understanding possible.

We are not the clothes we wear or the names we give ourselves. We are not the attributes of our bodies or the abilities we have or do not have. We do not define ourselves by what we may or may not be doing, thinking, or wearing, but we use these things as indicators to help us understand ourselves. We are more than the naked bodies we see in a bathroom mirror, in silhouette at night, or reflected in a pristine pool of water. We are more than what we see and what we feel and all that we think, but these are all parts and pieces of us. We may call this *me* or *I,* but these are all limitations that our ego minds can relate to and with. They may define us at specific points along our journeys, but they limit us. At some point, it becomes essential to abandon them so that we can become all that we choose to be. We reach new and greater understandings as we shed the clothes we used to wear and replace them with simpler and less-defining transparent apparel. We find beauty in transparent simplicity and celebrate life in all of its forms.

We search for meaning in things that have no meaning, and we place value on things that have no lasting value. The ego creates illusions of so-called success and failure and compares itself to the wine when it is the glass—and its purpose is to receive and be the glass. At some point, it reaches the lowest of lows and surrenders all of its attachments and fine clothes and replaces them with the transparent nakedness of the all-inclusiveness of love.

In this process, we do not *become* anything; we return to what we truly and already are. We return to love. If *honest* was one of the words we used to describe us, then we wouldn't become honest; instead, honest would become exposed as we allow it to shine through us. Love doesn't become honest because we use that word to describe it. It is impossible for it to become something that it already is or something that it is not.

During the process of abandoning the words that clothe and label us as things that we are not, we begin to shine the colors of love and shine the essence of us to all of creation. We call these colors *honesty, gentleness, kindness, infinite, eternal, forgiveness, respect, humor, fun, clarity, appreciation, understanding, faith, hope, charity, transparency, nakedness,* and more.

We can say that love is clothed in and with many things, and we can say that love is defined by all of its attributes, but in this, we limit it. It is more accurate to say that the attributes of love are defined by love. The clothes we wear, our hairstyles, and our eye colors do not define us. It is better to say that the clothes we wear are defined by who we think are and not what we wear. We make the shirt or sweater look good—and not the other way around. We define it with who we are. We make the hair or lack of it look good by returning to the love we naturally are.

We can say that love is clothed, but it is the love that defines the clothes because they merely highlight the form that is you. We can truly say they are transparent or maybe even see-through. Light isn't a rainbow, yet it defines the rainbow. The color white includes all of the other colors, but it isn't any of them. In contrast to this, darkness is the absence of light. Black is the absence of color, and evil is the absence of love. When we use love, our true essence, to define our clothes, we become filled with light. We become one with all of the colors that are full and overflowing with the endless possibilities that the universe has ready and waiting for us to claim. We become *free.*

As I clothe myself with harmony to the oneness of nature and surrender to the light, I realize that love is not clothed or defined by just one certain color. Just as the rainbow is clothed or defined by the light, all the colors of love are clothed and defined by the fullness of love. In a similar way, physical reality does not define who we are because we are clothed with love. It is our love that defines and clothes our physical reality. Love is the essence that clothes and defines us and all of creation.

I remember being present and one with the song of the bird. I didn't define the bird or the song, and they didn't define me, but we were defined by something that is unconditional and endless. Love contains and embraces all life. Love is, was, and will be the absence of limitations, and it fills all life with light.

Source breathes me and makes the force of gravity disappear. When I am happy, I am letting the colors of love shine through me. The brighter I allow them to be, the happier I am. The song tells me, without words, that I already have everything I need to be happy. I have my breath.

This is my ideal. I have lived a few moments of it here and there. May it always be my reality!

CHAPTER 7

Love Is Free

LOVE IS—IT JUST IS. LIKE gravity, it is one of those things that are self-evident. Love cannot be forced; it can only be gifted. It cannot be taken; it can only be received. Love is free to act, and it cannot be controlled. It cannot be made to be something it is not or made to do anything it isn't already doing. We can harmonize with it and work within its limitless creations, but we cannot put limits or conditions on it because it is free. We cannot use love to force or compel or cause another to do something they do not want to do because that is the absence of love.

What is free?

Rather than using a secondhand or thirdhand experience, I have chosen to give one from my personal life. This is one that I am comfortable with, and I have been able to use the sweetener of self-love in combination with the sting and sourness of the lemons of divorce and pressures of life to squeeze the juices from my soul to make delicious lemonade.

A week or two before my twentieth wedding anniversary, I had a divine impression that it is wrong to keep or force and mandate a person to be in a relationship they did not want to be in. I had to let her go. I had to let my wife go. I thought I knew what love was, but I began to learn how much I didn't know. Three months later, the divorce was final.

My life was forever changed, and it would never be the same. My boat had capsized, and my life raft was leaking and sinking fast. In my ego's selfishness, I wanted the appearance of freedom and the ability to dictate and control God to give me what I thought was love. I knew that I wasn't standing in my power, but I didn't know how that applied to all of life or even a small portion of it.

Words were said, and most were good. We committed to treat each other how we would like to treat the next person in our lives, which included completely giving of ourselves to each other with no conditions or limitations. The other thing I asked for was that we get our taxes done before any divorce papers were filed. These words sound pure and reasonable, but they had a hidden agenda. I was hoping that as she gave herself to me and the relationship in total completeness that she would fall in love with me again and that getting the taxes done would give us the time for that to happen—and that if that didn't work, then God would tell her to stay with me. My request wasn't free. It was attached to outcomes and control, and it was attached to my ego's self-preservation, which was interpreted as happiness.

It was a major challenge for me. For seven months, I went through cycles of letting go and then reattaching myself to desires to be with her. It was a time of darkness and the absence of light and self-love. I wanted to stand in my power, but I knew I wasn't doing it. I felt lost and directionless. I was in a thick fog on a moonless, overcast night. I felt like I was being acted on instead of being a participant in the action. It was like bondage, the absence of freedom. After seven months, I made the choice to completely let her go. I finally felt some freedom returning to me, and the weight of mental anguish and anxiety started to disappear.

I am now able to look at it as a valuable experience, but at the time, all I wanted was to be out of it. I wanted the pain to stop, and I wanted God to make it all better for me. Now, that behavior is repulsive and sickening to me.

When I let her go, who did I free? At first, I thought I was freeing her. In reality, I didn't. I freed *myself*. I freed myself from all the conditions and mandates I had in that area of my life. I freed myself from weakness and acts of non-love. I freed myself from expectations and the desire to please her or another in exchange for companionship and sex. I freed myself from being the victim.

Since then, I have had many more experiences in which I let go of different attachments and desires and wants. During each one, I experienced greater and greater freedom. With each one, I reclaimed and stood in my power a little more. I don't know if she felt free or anything like it; I never asked. Anything I could say about it would be my opinion and my view, and that changes according to where I may be standing in my journey. Did she make some choices because she didn't feel free? Did she feel like they were the only options she had at the time? I can't answer that, but I believe all of us have these feelings at some point in our lives.

With self-love, I freed myself. I cannot and could not cause anyone to feel free. I learned that love knows what could be, but it doesn't have to be it. At the same time, it sees our greatest potential. The feeling of freedom isn't caused by divorce; it isn't the result of leaving anyone. It sees the best in each other and what we can become. As it loves us *into* it, it loves us without expectations, conditions, mandates, or manipulative methods. It has no hidden agendas. Love is free of those methods of force, and when we act in and with love, we are free of those things.

Love cannot be used to act on others. It is acting with others; it is to be used to serve and bless and improve the lives and conditions of all, including within and around us. We can give a man a fish and feed him for a day or teach him how to fish and feed him for a lifetime. We can give a person love for a day with a love that comes and goes—or we can teach them to love themselves and make it last for a lifetime.

One of the best things I did was commit to mastering the voice in my mind to be empowering and loving. I guide it and use it, which empowers it to be creative and independent.

Love is more than a tool; it is the path to personal freedom. It guides and directs us, and at times, it even feels like it transfigures us to higher and greater abilities of life and more. Self-love includes commitment and compassion for ourselves and others, kindness, gentleness, self-forgiveness, forgiveness of others, understanding, acceptance, allowing, inclusion, trust, belief, and more. It is in and through the acts of self-love that we become free.

In the process of letting go, after the initial fear subsided, I felt like I was returning to love and to my true essence. I began to feel and see the different colors again. The brilliant tones of love blossomed, radiated, and shined from me. Just as the light by the door to your home illuminates the path, love invites us to come home, enter, and rest. It invites us to be born again into life with a new view of all that we are.

Love desires to be shared, and like the breeze, it can only be felt when we are in its flowing path. It is free of conditions and attachments, and it stands independently in its power. The ego creates attachments and conditions, and in creating these, it gives away our power to be free and to do and to act as one with the authentic songs of our hearts.

As I sought to regain and stand in my power, I learned that trying to please others and make them happy had discounted myself, which devalued them as well. By valuing myself—along with the limitless potential within me—I am increasing their value too. By seeing the best in me, I am able to open my eyes to see the best in you. I gradually expand it to see the best in everyone I meet. I learned that the ego creates the illusion of power at the expense of others with an arrogant attitude, which makes it impossible to feel the joy and bliss of being one with the song of life and love.

This doesn't mean that it is free of commitments, vows, kids, or relationships. It includes all of them. To be free of those things is like the ocean being free of all the fish and all the life it carries within it. It is free because it cannot be bought or sold. It is free because it cannot be asserted or forced into another's life. It is free because it can only be given and received as gifts of our truth. It moves among the rich and the poor as an equal. It doesn't judge or segregate. It isn't hostile or vengeful. It has no negative energies in it; in fact, the negative, low energy-imprisoning anxieties and heartbreaks are expressions of the absence of love. It isn't free sex with anything that breathes and has at least two legs and a mouth. It isn't fantasy and lust for the satisfaction of addictive physical pleasure. It is more than those, and it comes with lasting joy and happiness.

During the process of letting go of all attachments to my ex, I made some emotionally charged commitments that I thought would protect my heart and bring me love. At the time, I was acting from the false belief that love came from out there and that the purpose of marriage was for the wife to make the husband happy and for the husband to make the wife happy instead of being happy within and bringing love and joy into the relationship.

I had loved with all of my heart. I did things that I believed were love, but they actually were not. I did things like trying to make her happy as if I were her source of happiness. I did it with all of my heart. I hoped she would do the same for me, which is code for the ego trying to change another and to buy, sell, and barter for affection and attention in the name of love.

I complimented her, looked for the best in her, and trusted her even when I thought she was telling lies about me. I was hoping she would change and begin to treat me how I treated her. When I totally and completely let her go, I vowed that I would never give all of my heart to another until they gave me all of their heart first. That was another way of saying that I wanted them to be the leader instead of me. I was weak and powerless. I didn't want to trust others again, and I would wait to give them my trust and commitment until *after* they gave me theirs and proved to me with their actions that they were worthy of my love.

I thought I was somehow special and deserving of unconditional love, but my love was tainted with all kinds of conditions at the time. Every promise I made to myself during that segment of life was conditional on someone else's actions and responses to me. I falsely assumed that I could control how they felt about me by how I treated them. Every vow to myself at that time included limiting actions and beliefs. I gave my power to someone else. In essence, I was saying, "Hey, you be the leader because I'm weak, scared, and full of doubt. This is more about protecting the ego than giving anyone love—including you or me."

Within a few weeks, I began a series of events that lasted almost three years. I revisited, faced, and challenged each one of these ego-based mandates on myself and others. Some of these beliefs came from childhood, and others came from many years of marriage.

The first things I learned were that I had given away my power to be the leader of my life and the power to be happy. I immediately began removing those ego-based expectations from my life and replaced them with empowering ideas. As a result of being in a very low energy state, I was constantly looking for direction from external sources. They taught me that love is self-sufficient and looks within for the answers.

After a year, I realized I was only 98 percent committed to standing in my power and being free to love. The 2 percent that wasn't committed was destroying every relationship and all I desired. I remember the time and place when I became 100 percent determined to master the little voice in my mind. It was in the last couple of days of September, and my resistance made it tough as I repeatedly faced what felt like the impossible.

Each time I got back up, I felt myself standing a little taller. Each time required me to surrender a limiting false ego belief to the power and essence that is unconditional love. There was constant inner chaos and turbulence in my life; my problems and challenges were beyond my abilities back then. I instinctively knew I had to trust in this power in order to continue. At the time, my four kids—all between the ages of twelve and seventeen—were living with me 24/7.

Instinctively, I knew the best thing I could do for them was to be my best self. Gradually, during my greatest tribulations, I came to know that my greatest desire is to divinely guide and inspire the one I love to open and bloom into her greatest self. This is another way of saying to become and shine our divine perfection to all by being our better selves each day through living the way of happiness. I was working toward that ideal before the divorce came. As I held on to this desire, I went through another series of letting go of limiting desires and beliefs. Happiness became an everyday experience and began to fill each day.

I abandoned and replaced those limiting vows, commitments, and desires to please and look good with empowering ones. I committed to mastering my mind. I vowed to give myself self-love, to lead and guide by the example of standing in my power, to be the first to completely give all of my love in the relationship, and to lead the way by being in spirit so I could divinely guide and inspire my lover and family to open and bloom.

Love isn't limiting; it is freeing. As we abandon the limitations that we cover it with and return to the warmth and brilliance of the limitless abundance within us, it fills us with power and weightless freedom. Love is free to be one with the bird and to fly from earth to sky and back again. It is free to be one with the stream as it flows gently through a meadow or tumbles down a waterfall into a secluded pristine pool with the radiant sun blessing us with warmth and light. It is free to be one with the snowflake that lands on your nose as you make snow angels on a moonlit winter's night. And it is free for us to return to harmony with it—anytime and anyplace.

Pleasures can be bought and sold. Pleasures can be withheld and given and used to manipulate and blackmail. Lust and seduction, as exciting and erotic as they may be, are empty and shallow without love. The ego isn't free. It is controlled by desires for pleasure and many other things beyond its control, and it will use any method to get it, including drugs, pleasing others, mandates, and violence. The ego is addicted to pleasure and will choose it over happiness and promises to family as it seeks so-called happiness from things and lovers. The ego acquires or takes satisfaction in anger, resentment, remorse, self-pity, and holding grudges.

It resists compassion and forgiveness, which are essential parts of love.

Since love, in its essence, is naked, it exposes everything for what it truly is: the real thing or an imposter. The ego imposter will go to extremes to prove that it is real and that it is the creator of all that is good in our lives and that everything that is bad or undesirable is the creation of others or evil. Since the essence of love reveals and exposes true reality, the ego resists the path of freedom. In order to become free of the limiting beliefs, I had to admit that I was wrong and see each one in its nakedness for what it really is or isn't.

Love is free of self-pity, which empowers it to be free to be compassionate. Love is free of segregation because love is *inclusion*. Love is free of remorse and resentment because love is being understanding. It is free of negativity because it is all that is good. Love is free of anger and violence because love is *accepting, allowing,* and *forgiving.* Love is free of everything that brings us down because it empowers and lifts. It is free of oppression, mandates, blackmail, despair, aggression, anxiety, scorn, hate, envy, vengeance, apathy, fear, demands, guilt, shame, evil, blame, carelessness, self-deprivation, superiority, regrets, endless grief, withdrawal, and enslavement. It is free of anything and everything that sucks the energy out of us and anything that will bring us down. Love is free of the forces that consume energy because it is power. Love is self-sustaining and permanent. It is stationary and invincible.

Love, in its freedom, supports and flows through all life. Unconditional love is endless in its presence and its brilliance. It is complete with intense beauty and perfection, and it radiates the joy of its divine essence in and through all of creation. It is something that cannot be seen. Like the flowing stream and the sweet song of the bird at sunrise, love is an experience that breathes life into all who are one with it. Love is experienced, and as we participate in the oneness of it, it illuminates us and shines a unique and mysteriously intoxicating brilliance of warmth, peace, and life through us. We see beauty in everyone and everything.

Love is complete and needs nothing to make it whole or fill it. It is free to say, "I already have everything I need in order to be happy." Love *does*—and it is meaningful, harmonious, and hopeful. Love empowers, trusts, and forgives. Love is optimistic. Love understands, respects, and has reverence for other people and nature. It accepts, allows, includes, completes, and fills us. It gives life meaning and satisfaction, and it teaches and illuminates the paths of our journeys as we choose the way of happiness.

Love empowers us to commit and enter into vows *with* each other instead of *to* each other. It teaches us how to become whole as a wineglass is whole, complete, and empty all at the same time. It teaches us how to be the wine and how to fill another's glass. Love teaches us that we are complete in our own identity, and it is in coming together as the wine and chalice through sharing with each other that deeper completion in which our oneness is discovered.

Love is free, and it makes us free when we harmonize with it and invite it to shine from and through us. It is in you and in me in equal portions. The more we seek it and harmonize with it, the more we experience and feel it. This takes commitment and dedication. It isn't for the weak of heart. Many times, we need a helping hand along the way to show us how to love in unconditional ways. The companion in a committed relationship can be the best helping hand we ever have.

Love is free in its authentic nakedness and clothed in illuminating transparency.

SECTION III

One

CHAPTER 8

Love Is Surrender

The thing we surrender to becomes our power.

—Ernest Holmes

SURRENDERING TO UNCONDITIONAL LOVE REQUIRES an unconditional commitment to loving ourselves.

I like who I am. The thought of changing just to make another person happy just feels off and out of harmony with my Source, because we can never change who we *truly* are. At the same time, it is important to remember that as we stand in our power, we abandon the idea of attaching our identity to what we do, what we eat, where we are from, what we look like, and anything that limits us and our dreams. Be gentle, let go of the lowest feelings first, and do it with self-love. Our view of who we are—the things we identify with—is constantly evolving, but it never changes who we are.

The summer of 2007 is etched deeply into my mind.

It was the end of June, the heat was intense, and we were working in Anderson, California. The days were long— thirteen to fifteen hours a day—in the direct sunlight. The temperatures were up to 115 degrees Fahrenheit, and we were working with reflective metals. The second night, I went to bed feeling good and looking forward to a restful sleep on a pleasant summer night. Life was improving and looking up, and I had a good attitude. Within an hour of going to sleep, I woke up in sickening fear from a dream that still carries an emotional charge.

I dream in vivid color, and I sometimes have several dreams per night. There have been phases of my life when I dream things that happen later that day or week; sometimes it is a month or a couple years later. This happens several times a year, and to me, it is ordinary and natural. In fact, I used to think everyone had dreams like that in the same way I did.

That night's dream was more emotionally packed than any I have had since the age of ten. It began wonderfully; in my dream, the weather was perfect, my health was great, I had friends and family, and I was surrounded by those who loved me. I couldn't see them, but I knew they were there. The only people in the dream were my three closest friends and me. I saw them in the distance, and as we came together, I was expecting hugs and love. Instead, they were determined to destroy me, annihilate me, and exterminate me. They did not just want to destroy my body and physical life; they wanted to annihilate my entire existence and presence and everything that was related to me.

I have never had the fear of physical death; death has always felt like a temporary condition like moving to a different city or country. I know we will eventually meet again. I do have phobias about pain and getting hurt—but not about dying. That dream was more than death; it was the total and complete annihilation of my essence, which gives me life and allows me to think, breathe, and have an identity. They weren't asking me to surrender; they were out to destroy my source with force, seduction, deceit, and any other method they could think of. I somehow escaped them, and the dream ended. I woke up in a state of extreme fear. My heart was racing, and I knew I had just barely escaped total obliteration.

I stayed awake for hours. I was too afraid to sleep. For days, it took focus and meditation to overcome the fear that came at night. The only part that involved surrender was the surrendering of the fear as I lay down to sleep. Love defends and protects life; instead of attacking it, it will reach out to heal. Instead of destroying life, it will create. Instead of force, ultimatums, threats, and take-it-or-leave-it and my-way-or-the-highway attitudes, it encourages, empowers, accepts, allows, includes, gives, guides, and inspires.

As the ego takes away life, love gives new life. It refills us, energizes us, and gives us another chance to be a little better. The dream filled me with fear, but love guided me to let go, to surrender, and to be supported in love. Love gave me hope when fear had taken it away.

In order to sleep, I had to ignore the endless scenarios and debates about what the future misfortunes might be. In place of them, I listened to the soft words coming from within. They came from a place close to my heart. It includes my heart, but it is not my physical heart. It came from a place that is deep and has no limits in its goodness. Like many other good experiences, I am still looking for the words to describe the life that comes with it.

Many intense moments have come, including having my heart shocked back into rhythm and being told more than once that my odds of living for more than a couple more months were very slim if at all. All those experiences—as challenging and emotionally packed as they were—do not come close to the intensity of that dream and the impact it had on me. I would never wish that experience on anyone.

Almost a year later, I was in Miami with one of my three friends from the dream. I still consider them friends. We had been studying hypnosis and its benefits. I had gone through an experience with hypnosis where my good side saw and experienced my dark side. Instinctively, I knew that in order to be complete and be whole, both parts of my identity needed to be embraced. If the struggle continued, the darkness would overshadow and cloud the light. Ignoring the undesirable was not an option anymore. The time had come for me to make a stand, and I didn't like what I saw. It was very destructive, strong, and forceful. I wanted to be free of it, but that was impossible. I wanted to kill it, but the more I resisted it and fought it, the stronger it became. It already appeared to be stronger than my good side.

I eventually realized that I had to surrender to it in love with love. I thought that my personality would change and that I would be different, redefined, or transformed. I thought I might even become evil. I thought I might die; in fact, I was sure that some part of me would die. Since I had a friend with me, I was inspired to continue and to surrender in and with love completely to the dark side of me, which was blacker than anyone I knew or knew of.

In this hypnotic state, I saw myself lay down in complete submission as I allowed the dark me to engulf my total self. The dark soul was devoid of light and love. It was cold because there was no warmth in its soul, and it sucked the energy and power out of all life. I allowed it to come over me. It felt suffocating and deathly. I felt it melting into me and taking me over as it pushed out the life and all that was good. The light began to disappear.

As my last breath came, just before the dark force overcame me, a power flowed in that I can only describe as light, life, warmth, joy, mercy, power, acceptance, and love. This living power flowed into me and through me. It surrounded me. It destroyed the dark master with the total inclusion of love, and all his dark power was transformed to good. Healing replaced death; warmth and love replaced or filled the absence and voids of all that had been ruled by coercion, blackmail, assertion, and force. I was filled with life, and the darkness and oppression were replaced with light, acceptance, and allowing. Peace and tranquility filled me, and for a moment, time stopped.

After all this, I had the feeling of having traveled through many lifetimes, and then I returned to the present. Many details have been left out, and a book could be written about this one experience, which only lasted for an hour. For the next two weeks, the peace I had experienced stayed with me. It continued to grow for a short time.

In the dream, there are some things that show what surrendering is not. It doesn't happen with force; in fact, the more force and resistance there is, the bigger the unwanted entity becomes. In the hypnotic state, the more I resisted and fought against my dark side, the bigger it became.

The more we resist and oppose the ego's desires, the bigger they become. It is impossible to end conflict with conflict or end war with war; it is impossible to end peace with peace and love with love. The more we oppose opposition with opposition, the more opposition we receive.

When we surrender the desire to oppose and turn or

respond in ways that are empowering and inclusive, we can stand in our power, which is different than wimpy submission and a pleasing-you-at-any-cost attitude. When we choose to stand in our power, we are acting in spirit.

Look around, watch the news, read the paper, or talk to the friend who is getting a nasty divorce. Conflicts, wars, and spiteful divorces all have one thing in common: they are missing and devoid of love and peace. They thrive on proving themselves right at any cost. Not all divorce situations are spiteful; some are in the best interests of everyone. There are those who can be great friends but not be married.

The only way to end war is to break the cycle by being peaceful, which involves surrendering our prejudices and superiorities and replacing them with the power of acceptance, inclusion, and allowing. This doesn't mean not defending our freedoms; it is saying that there are better ways than violence and opposition by finding and developing those powers.

The wind doesn't ask the tree to move or the mountain to be different, but it shapes the tree, and as it goes around the mountain, it polishes and smooths the rough places. Harmony is created as both parties surrender to compassion and the commitment to us, forgiveness, allowing, and acceptance.

The war within me between the dark and the light grew larger the more I resisted; it ended when the light side surrendered in love to becoming one (inclusion) with the dark side. The dark side will never surrender; it will always resist and claim the power that it appears to take from others. It controls the ego in varying degrees. In order to survive, the dark side attempts to take power from others because it isn't self-sufficient like love is. It is devoid of intrinsic power, and in the place of this power, it uses force as it pretends it is all-powerful.

The way to end peace is to take it away with anxiety, turmoil, chaos, distress, and the black holes that represent the absence of love. If we want peace in our lives, we must surrender or let go of *anything* that opposes peace. We must surrender to peace. Some have said that we surrender everything over to peace, but that can be misleading. The mind takes everything literally, and it feels off track to surrender everything when all we are do is let go of the opinions of the ego. We can keep our identities and everything else that empowers us to love. The only things that we let go of are those that discount our true essence and withhold love from our lives and the lives of others. As we yield or turn over anything that opposes peace, we learn that peace empowers us. In a sense, it is now our power because it is us and we are it. When we want love in our lives, we must surrender to love with love.

I've seen too many self-righteous wannabe men who deliberately twist these ideals to justify their desire to manipulate and control women and children to become objects and things. If that were the darkest hour of it, then it wouldn't be as sad and obscene as it is for too many people. There are many people in the world who have been sexually abused. Many surrendered their pain, anguish, and all their dark and lonely nights. They surrendered those pains to forgiveness, found power, and discovered the power within themselves to heal and to love. They are now able to stand in their power to love and forgive.

Joy, peace, and love are found in the present moment. I used to live in the future, which brings anxiety and fear. Much of it had to do with my position at work—making schedules, ordering supplies, looking at deadlines, and meeting commitments—and trying to squeeze in family time. The feeling of missing out on life consumed me.

When the mind wasn't in the future, it was in the past, which brings depression and regret. I tried to remember why I was doing what I did—and I remembered better times—as I tried to escape the so-called reality in its unpleasantness. I increasingly turned over the habit of being in the future and the past to be present with life and to the giving of self-love. In that way, I found love within me along with the satisfactions that flow with it.

Over the years, my ego created some attachments to being right. It thought those things were the foundation of the happy, fulfilled life. I had strong attachments to opinions, positions, and views, and some of them were very harsh and condemning.

At one time, I even identified with the drama in my life. I was attached to it. For many years, my life and ego were devoid of the concept of self-love. I constantly beat the love right out of me. I repeatedly attempted to give love without giving self-love to me. It was impossible. Gradually, over a few years, this changed and I began to love life and myself.

Devotion to unconditional love guarantees unconditional mercy: mercy to yourself and to your ego, mercy to each other, and mercy to your families and to others. It includes giving self-love no matter what. Surrendering to unconditional love requires an unconditional commitment to loving yourself. Sacrifice your doubts and fears by replacing them with love and belief.

When we surrender to passion, we become gently passionate. We also become everything that we surrender to in the way that we do it. If we were to surrender in force to passion, we would become forcefully passionate. If a person attempts this process with rigid requirements and deadlines, they will self-destruct.

When we want passion in our lives, we must apply it with love. When we want order, we must let go of all the mandates and reorganize in the naked transparency of love. When we want peace, we must apply peace in loving ways.

Force can bring seasons of the absence of war that may resemble peace, but it can never bring peace. I can make my kids sit next to each other and not fight and even go through the motions of showing affection with a hug, but I can't force them to feel peace and love for each other. There are many different methods or qualities of love, and they are all good; eventually, they all may become our power.

I am still working on yielding to chaos in love. When I come home and find the kitchen in shambles, the living room is a war zone, and it gets more chaotic with every step, it is hard to let go of the desire to dictate every move of every kid until it is all clean and just love them in the messy, chaotic moment. And yet, every time I let go of the desire to organize the chaos and just love them in the moment and love the moment, it seems as if everything reorganizes in wonderful ways.

Love is surrender is accurate only when we surrender with love to qualities of love and to all that is one with it. It is going along with nature that is already perfect in every way because it is already one. Submitting to the desire to be or to do, embracing the *now* of each moment as the one thing that is real, and becoming one with the transparent nakedness of love is surrendering in love.

Emotions are our friends; they guide us to the ecstasy of love. For years, I avoided them, despised them, and ignored them. The tiny world I grew up in viewed emotions as wimpy or weak. They were distractions that caused pain, unmanly, and an enemy of all that is good. Some went as far as to say that they came from the devil to seduce us and lead us to our destruction. If I wanted to be respected as a man, every emotion had better be suppressed. Everything I did had to have a logical reason and motive that came from the head, and the creative way of the heart could never be mentioned.

I was taught that it wasn't manly to write, be compassionate, or be an artist, actor, painter, or musician. Those were all emotional, and that was worse than bad. To live this lie requires that any and every time an emotion begins to emerge that we suppress it by either pushing our way out of it by pushing into the future or by pulling ourselves out of it by pulling back into the past. For many years, I thought being emotionless meant suppressing emotions and not allowing them to surface. This definition is more like apathy and a state of numbness with the shock of despair instead of the happiness and love that is independent and unattached to desires and outcomes. It allows us to breathe and be filled with the cycles of the emotions of creation.

When I began to allow the truth that emotions are my friends and embraced them, I found it very uncomfortable. At first, I wouldn't let them stay. After a second or two, I would jump into the future because it was too uncomfortable to be present with them. Then I thought I was avoiding the unpleasant or bad emotions—and it would be easy to embrace to good ones—but that wasn't the case. As I focused on accepting them, I jumped out of the good ones sooner than the unpleasant ones. I don't know why I did it, but I know that I did and where I went.

I slowly developed the ability to ride the wave and just experience them as pleasant or unpleasant, neither good nor bad, with something to offer me. In my resistance, it was difficult to change the way I looked at them and view them like a painting with vibrant contrasting colors. Each color was necessary to complement and bring out the beauty and feeling of the moment. I looked at them as an elaborate mosaic with fine details. If one tile or piece was ignored or missing, the story would be left unfinished.

I listened to the dissonance in the music and saw how the unpleasant sound added to the harmony of the next phrase. I could see how each color of the rainbow is equal even though I prefer some more than others. I applied this same thought to my emotions to assist me in opening my arms to my life and lovingly embraced it with all of the contrast that comes my way.

Today, much of the sting has disappeared from the unpleasant experiences. I have let go of attachments to outcomes and desires for things to be certain ways. I have been able to ride many of my emotional waves to their completion; some of them have been larger than I thought I could handle. It has turned out to be very fulfilling and much better than I thought it would be.

In all of this, I never surrendered who I am just to become something different. If anything, I became more like me. It was like I came home and stopped pretending to be something I wasn't. I have the feeling of being free to be authentic, which allows me to be vulnerable with you.

I sacrificed and handed over the desire to escape into the past or the future so I can be present in the moment with the one I love, with nature, and with everything else that is one in perfection. I remembered that in all the times I had been one with nature, I was in a sense emotionless because I was one with all that emotion attempts to define but can't because it constantly evolves.

Every snapshot of my existence contains a variety of emotions, depending on how they are perceived. I allow myself to feel and experience every emotion in its fullness, and all of them eventually transform to become pleasant. I know that some emotions are only the absence of love: hate, envy, despair, vengeance, segregation, and worthlessness. I learned that the greater the contrast, the more I could feel love. I can go deeper in both my light and dark sides, I can go deeper with you or anyone else, and I can stay present in the hurricanes of relationships and intimacy.

It is much easier to ride the bull and get kicked in the head than it is to be present and go deep into the abyss of the emotional storm that is just part of nature. I no longer need to change how the sun shines or the wind blows; it is perfect as it is, and all that needs to be done is to allow the moment to carry me, breathe me, and fill me with the love of life as these words become reality: "All I need is the air that

I breathe and to love." It can be you, another, or something else—as long it includes self-love.

Surrender the ego's desires and master the mind in love with self-love. When we love ourselves in completeness, we are ready to embrace our lovers in completeness. Don't wait until some future unknown date to make that commitment or to give that love. Begin now, make mistakes, cause a storm, and practice relaxing into the chaos with self-love. It will come. Commit in the fear of committing, love in the fear of loving, surrender in the fear of surrendering, and trust and know that when we do it in love and in harmony with the inner voice that speaks from the core of our hearts, it will be good for us—even when it doesn't feel like it at the time.

Love is surrendering to being your better self. It isn't pushing or pulling, it isn't resisting or opposing, and it isn't imposing. Like embracing my dark side, it is including all of me so I can be all I can be. It is surrendering part of what we thought we were so we can be whole—like a complete day includes darkness and light, storms and rainbows, and the valleys and mountains and plateaus and mesas. It is embracing all of me so I can embrace all of you in your storms and seasons of blooming from the deepest inferno to the highest ecstasy. It is surrendering to *us* in love of each other. It isn't committing to one or the other at the expense of our own identities. The inclusion of each other gives us the power to make us feel more like our individual selves in the freedom of the *oneness of us*.

CHAPTER 9

One

DICHOTOMY IS A DIVISION OR contrast between two things that are not the same or are represented as being opposed to each other or entirely different. We have been taught to look at much of life as opposite and opposing forces when, in fact, they are part of the same entity. There are masculine and feminine, hot and cold, black and white, up and down, positive and negative, heads and tails, front and back, and beginnings and endings. The list continues. There may be dichotomy in some things, but most, if not all of the things the ego refers to as opposites and opposing are actually complementary expressions of each other. In many ways, they define what the other is.

Take a beginning and an ending. They are both a point of view that we use to describe something in relation to us, or a direction we are going, to represent time and place. We can begin in the present and end in the past or in the future. We can begin on the left or the right and end in the middle.

We use beginnings and endings to help us understand the endless by taking pictures of time with a beginning and an ending. We talk about heads and tails of a coin as if they are two separate coins or even as opposing sides instead of complementary pieces (not opposites) of the same unit. Hot and cold and up and down are in relation to some random object that we use to explain what we want. The temperature of a cold shower is much different than a cold day or a cold drink. They are different parts or places that we choose to help us define life and the moment.

In school, I was taught that the positive and negative sides of a magnet were opposites. It was defined in such a way that made it appear as if they were separate identities that couldn't exist together as one. The confusion came from their lack of understanding, which kept the ignorance going. In order for a magnet to be a magnet, it must have the complementary yin and yang, the masculine and feminine, the positive and the negative. They are not opposites; they are interconnected aspects and qualities of the same entity or power. People have referred to them as opposites in an attempt to define individual threads of life in an attempt to help us understand and recognize what we think is the whole picture.

In order for us to have a three-dimensional life, we need limits and contrasts for our minds to comprehend. There is no need for opposites; we don't need yellow to be opposite of anything for it to be yellow or for blue or red to be opposite of anything. However, we refer to black and white as opposite when we know they are really already perfect as they are. They are just different. There is no good or bad in the way a color looks; there is only personal taste and preference. In the magnet, there is no right or wrong in being positive or negative. They both attract ferrous metals like iron. They are both part of the same unit; in order for one side to exist, the other side needs to exist. They complement and define each other. They are each other's yin and yang—and maybe they *zing* when they come together.

For years, I have heard that the man needs the woman in order to be whole and the woman needs the man. Those same people attempt to define them as opposites and opposing forces, and they use those misleading beliefs to justify using manipulative force to make the other be the same as they are and ignore the feminine and masculine gifts. Their definitions make it almost impossible to be one even though, by nature, we are already one. We devote so much of life to defining how we are different, and in the act of resisting happiness, they state how right they are.

The book of Genesis teaches that we are one, we come from the same source, and we are to help each other. That sounds like we are equals to me. If we had two differently shaped wineglasses—and one was shaped like a man and the other like a woman—and then we filled them with wine from the same bottle, would the wine be better in one because it looked different? You may say one is better because it holds more, but that has nothing to do with the taste of the wine or the shape of the glass.

Men and women have all of the masculine and feminine traits. A magnet has the positive and negative poles in every part of it, and if we were to break a piece of it off, it would make two complete individual magnets—each with its own positive and negative sides. We have choice. We also have a divine essence within us that is either masculine or feminine in its nature. We can choose to express one more than the other or both. We can try to ignore our natural polarity at the expense of authentic freedom—or we can just let it come out. Many in our society who think they are just letting it come out are often taking on or developing true aspects of the authentic self at the expense of devaluing other intrinsic qualities of their authentic self, which makes their polarity stagnate and become weaker.

When I became a single parent, I thought I could be the mom and the dad. I tried for a few months, and then I realized that was not my path. In order to be me and stand in my true power, I had to be masculine. I could be a great dad—but not a mom. I chose to be masculine because that is what my divine essence is, and I am happy in that. However, that does not mean I can't be kind, compassionate, loving, caring, fun, forgiving, accepting, and spontaneous. All of these traits are both masculine and feminine.

I have seen many people, mostly women, take on both the yin and the yang of human essence and then wonder what happened after they became the man buddy and their femininity became neutral. They are trying to live a role that they are not, and that takes the zing out of life and any relationship. I wanted my daughter and three sons to see what it means to be a man's man. Society already has more than enough examples of force and imposters. I told them that I was their dad and that I wouldn't pretend to be a mom or anything other than a dad. Sometimes our house looked more like a bachelor pad than a home. It would have been nice to have the feminine touch that gives added warmth. They have learned that cooking, dishes, laundry, and yard work are all part of life and not the role of either the man or the woman. It is both. The masculine stands firm, but it can bend with love to meet the storms and demands of life.

They have their complementary opposites and their own positive and negative personalities. At eight years old, my daughter began writing me notes. Within an hour, they could go from me being the best dad in the world to the worst and then back to the best. With each change in the tide—no matter what the notes said—I stood firm in my love, thanked her for the note, and said, "I love you too." Since then, I have been hated, disowned, despised, and above all, loved and wanted.

Remember that we can be both sides of the magnet but not

at the same time. Some of the negative traits are controlling, dominating, manipulating, forceful, and being what we call a jerk or other degrading names. The feminine side looks more like the hippie sex-drug-love-peace movement with no commitment to anything, including Source, and it seeks freedom in temporary pleasures. These make it challenging to create a strong relationship.

Most of the positive traits are similar: freedom in commitment to each other and Source, lifting each other, allowing, being open-minded, and being gentle. When both sides have the positive traits, it is easy to become one.

Father Time is dependable and steady and never changes. Mother Nature is unpredictable and can let loose a storm now and then. To be one with each other is to bring all of you and all of me to the table: the dark, the light, the good, the bad, the ugly, and the love. The feminine seeks divine guidance from her man, and if he can't give it or chooses not to give it, she will go to another for it. It is the role of the man to divinely guide and inspire the woman, and that requires him to be in spirit. It requires him to be constantly evolving toward his better self, leaning just beyond his comfort zone, and staying present in every situation.

He brings purpose to the relationship and leads with the words: "Come follow me." He *invites* her to journey with him. He is to stand steady in his power during the storms that threaten to destroy and annihilate all that they have created—and give her unconditional love, inspire her, and guide her to safety in love as he stays present while facing his worst fears and nightmares. All the while, he knows the best gifts he can receive from her are her tests that constantly refine him with both the pleasant and the unpleasant and allow him to be his better self. In his steadiness, he is immovable—yet he is open-minded and gentle and embraces all. He listens to her words, values them, and then makes a decision based on all the information he has. He doesn't compromise to please her or anyone else, yet he includes them. If she instinctively senses that he is slacking, she will be repulsed by it—and the feminine storms will come.

This is life. Live it fully and love it completely. Embrace it and become one together in it as *us*. It is about discovering all that we have in common and using our personal colors to color with each other to make a portrait of one called *us*. It is about allowing and accepting diversity as we include each other with committed hearts and souls. It is about him being the wineglass that is whole yet empty to receive the feminine wine of life. It is about her being the wine that intoxicates him with her beauty and love as it refreshes, energizes, and empowers him to self-mastery and personal discovery. It gives him the confidence to walk erect through life.

It is about them being complete and whole in their true essence and becoming one together to be even greater as one with each other. Somewhere along the path, we discover how to be one with the song of the bird as the breeze adds its voice to the melody. In storm or paradise, and all that is between, we discover that it is possible to become one in all that life has to offer. It inspires and empowers us to use every color to add beauty and contrast to our mosaic of life.

May we be one! It is our birthright!

CHAPTER 10

Love Is Sex

WHEN DOES IT BEGIN? WHEN does it end? Can we be in love and not know it? When is it mutual? Does it end with death? Did it begin before birth? Is it possible or necessary to answer these questions? Some would say that if it has a beginning, then it has an ending. I disagree with that. I think that once love between a man and a woman has become one, then it has no end. That commitment is created by choice through free will between two people along with our divine Source.

When does it begin? It is like the flower; does the flower bloom when the bud first shows its color or when it has fully opened? Does the breeze begin to blow when we first feel it or before it reaches us? It doesn't matter because we have choice. We can choose as a couple to water the flower of love and nourish it; as long as we are united, it will continue to evolve and blossom. As soon as one decides to withdraw their love, the plant begins to die. Maybe one of them can keep it alive for an indefinite amount of time, but unless they reunite their love, it will eventually lose its color and give way to another.

In death, when one of us appears to die, the love can continue because there is only love for each other in the nonphysical realm. I think we can wake up one morning and realize that we have been in love for a month or a year and didn't know it. There can be times when what we thought was love was actually emotional attachments built on the insecurities of neediness and lust in that moment. We can take the higher road of love and choose together to transform the physical passion of lust and physical desire into more as we come together in physical intimacy with the desire to become one in every way.

Too often, romantic love is shown as the knight in shining armor rescuing the damsel in distress and taking away all of the problems of life, and they live happily ever after with no more storms to disturb their perpetual bliss. There is also the woman who takes on the charity case, and as she nurses him to health, *she* transforms him. All *his* destructive habits just disappear because of her love for him. And there is the peasant who becomes the queen and much more.

Many of the traits shown are love, including seeing the best in the one we are with and believing and trusting in them—even when they doubt themselves. It is misleading when their happiness is dependent upon who they are with, physical conditions being perfect, and believing that once love is found then there are no more challenges in life.

Cinderella was happy and loved life before any of the wonderful things came to her. Her evil stepsisters were jealous of her happiness, but there was nothing they could do about it. They tried to suck her into their pit of despair and misery. Snow White brought joy and beauty everywhere she went, and the storms of life couldn't keep her down. This is healthy self-love and they found their zing in Prince Charming, and he was also happy and passionate in life in spite of the challenges in his path.

Beauty and the Beast shows how to see the best in another and give love no matter what with no thought of being loved by the selfish beast. At first, she didn't like him, but as she chose to serve and be compassionate, she began to give of herself. Eventually, he opened his heart, received her love, and chose to sacrifice his beastly ways for those of love. It took time and persistence. She didn't do it to win his love or to make him be something different than he was. He didn't have to change, and the space was created where it could be, but it didn't have to be the love story of all time. No one knows when it became love or when it became mutual; only they know that it is. It took both people and a commitment, and even though it may have begun as a one-sided, lustful, possessive relationship, Beauty had the power to see the best in the beast and to bring it out by encouraging the beast in her man to become his better self. There were many nights that she wanted to give up and run away. There was no knight in shining armor to take away all the problems and *make* her happy. She developed happiness within as she chose to love. It took self-love and commitment. It took all that she had and more; it took her life energy, and then she received it all back and much more.

What is love? Is it the sex, the touch, the time together, or what? There are books about the different languages of love that teach us how to speak it without saying a word. There are books about how to put the zing into our romance in and out of the bedroom. We can zing with many different people and feel it on different levels and not have sex with them. We can take those moments and add them to becoming one with the one we have vowed to dream with as we walk together through the ups and downs of life. We can take each spark of lust and love and gift it to each other through emotion, touch, and the honesty of loving sex with our partner with the desire to be *us*, to be one with each other.

Love is always complete in the moment and never lacking, but we are always evolving in the ability to completely love. When we come together in marriage and vow to dare to dream together as we ride the waves of insanity that leave us naked in ecstasy on the beaches of life, we have no idea of the inconvenience or the darkness of the winter storms—and we blindly say yes.

Divorce, broken promises, lies in the night as we touch, and relationships that were once filled with trust and then ended in betrayal all teach us that self-love is our primary source of happiness and that it is foolish to look for anyone or anything to give us the feeling of love. We feel the instinct to share ourselves and connect with others through sex. Some have sex through acts of non-love. Love is totally absent as they manipulate and force themselves on others.

There are those who have twisted the truth that sex is holy into the idea of holy sex with children and prostitutes and other acts that are devoid of love. Some purchase it for the pleasure and ecstasy of orgasmic lust. Others sell their bodies for the nights of physical highs without commitment and continue their lonely lives without knowing how much more fulfilling it could be. Many have become dissatisfied because of their companions' lack of commitment to truth in the acts of intimacy in the bedroom, and they have chosen to withhold their vulnerable nakedness of love. They attempt love in sex and choose not to commit to each other for various reasons, but they seek companionship and the energy of erotic touch as they share a portion of themselves with each other.

Then there are those who love with open transparency as they gift all of their innermost secrets and deepest desires to each other through the oneness and "us-ness" of sex. In this act, sex becomes love and love becomes sex.

In the silence the love grows strength, truth, and honesty in the night. There are no lies to whisper there; commitment is in the heart, bound to trust all that is.

In openness and truth, we come together to gift all of me to you and all of you to me with no limitations. We allow the dark and the light to merge and become one. We meet each other as equals and let the zing of our masculine and feminine attractions create waves of ecstasy that may threaten to destroy our unity. And as the angel of the light along with the dark temptress of destruction within the feminine, she meets her man who is willing to go with her in every extreme. He approaches life the same way he makes love with her: with passion and zest for life in the present moment. Loving with immovable, open gentleness that includes all and allows each wave to rise from the bottomless abyss and then leads it to its greatest moment. He bends and dances with her life energy as he becomes one with her ever-changing moods.

Her deep feminine energy refines and gives him strength as long as he stays present with love. In oneness, he leads and guides her to stay open, and the storm is replaced with the tranquility of his open heart. They go for a walk in the park, along the creek, or on the beach; it doesn't matter where or what they do because they are one together. Love is watching the sun setting and the clouds changing colors, it is melting together in openness within the truth of the erotic moment as we come together, and it is combining the song of your wine to become one with my glass in the silence of the moment. It is allowing the pressure of the storm of the temptress to squeeze the sour juice from the lemon into the water of life and then guiding the angel of light to sweeten it with her love, making sweet lemonade to refresh our hearts and souls.

Love is many things. When we add commitment to become one with another, with each other as *us*, it reveals itself in greater depth and detail. It takes on deeper meaning as it reveals itself to us. We see it in all of its splendor and beauty, empowering us to deeply experience the intoxicating tranquility of love, and then love as sex becomes an open path for us to mesh as one with each other in every way and at the same time retain our individual colors.

Is it possible to keep the zing in a relationship and become one? Is it possible to breathe the same air and eat the same food and be one and yet keep our individual identities? Magnets are weak when their positive and negative charges are in chaos, but when they are aligned with their attractive power, they grow strong and increase in power.

When there is chaos without alignment, they have lost zing and attractiveness and are not magnets anymore. The greater their alignment, the more powerful the attraction or the zing in the relationship. Real zing is a link between two people that flows energy without conscious effort and has a connection that feels in a way like home. Looks have little to do with it. It is like an instinct or a reflex that acts on its own. It can be ignored but not suppressed. From my perspective, it makes what some would call an average-looking person become more beautiful than Aphrodite, the goddess of love. This connection is intuitive, it is felt and experienced, and it is amazing. It is a taste of becoming one, and it can develop and grow as two evolve together. It breathes us, moves us, and binds us as one. It is the path to being *us*—to you feeling what I feel and me feeling what you feel. It is being individuals who are inseparably connected. It is the connection that lets you know everything about me. It can feel like a surge of energy flowing through your body. It is all of these and more, and I am looking forward to experiencing it more as it intensifies in my life.

When we exchange vows, we determine that if either of us feels this with another person in stronger ways than how we are experiencing it together in our relationship that we will learn how to create and empower our zing to become more powerful between us than any other person we meet. We will use the zings that we feel with other people to add to ours and to promote oneness with each other. If and when we do experience this with another, then we will embrace and savor the flow of energy without sex and then express it with our lover through sex and other actions.

To keep this magnetism alive, it is imperative and crucial

that we live our masculine and feminine essence in alignment and harmony with our Source of life and power. If I were to take the storms out of Mother Nature, there would be no waves of ecstasy to ride, and each climax would get smaller and smaller until they were just ripples in a small pool of complacency within companionship. If that is what others are looking for, then they can have it. I want attractiveness and a woman who inspires me in all of her moods, dark and light. I want one who can take me places I have never been before. At the same time, she is willing to follow me on the path of inspiration and unconditional love—while being spontaneous and crazy enough to love me with complete openness within the privacy of our home. She will share me with everyone and is jealous enough to keep me all to herself, and as she allows me the freedom to be my authentic self, she embraces me with unconditional love in every moment.

As we come together, we surrender to each other and to the idea of us. The woman surrenders to the masculine to feel his inner strength and guidance as he harmonizes with the divine; the man surrenders to the feminine as she frees her dark angel to seduce him to ride the feminine storm and discover how to divinely guide and inspire her to be the angel of light within her soul. The wineglass surrenders to its emptiness so it can receive the intoxicating song of the goddess, and in turn, the wine surrenders its form to be held by the chalice; together, they are one as they share all that they are with the world in their own unique way.

People dream, people dare, people want to believe, and people dare to dream together. They vow, "From this day forward, I will dream with you, dare with you, and want with you, and it will be you and me." You voice it, and perhaps a few are invited to witness it. It isn't convenient, and it takes commitment beyond our understanding. The vows were said, but it didn't happen instantly; it took time for the rough edges to be polished in the storms of life. You did it without knowing what all was involved, and you would do it again.

God intends for love to be mutual and for us to be one. Sometimes when we think about these ideals, it feels uncomfortable. We may question if we have what it takes—or if we even want to go the distance. Intuitively we know that the one who loves the most and lets go of their natural animal ego (the beast in *Beauty and the Beast*) is the one who inspires others. They are willing to appear crazy. They are crazy enough to believe they can change the world, and they actually do. They change their world and the world of their lover and all those they meet. The feminine find this attractive and beautiful while asking for kindness, gentleness, compassion, and every form of love that the masculine has to offer in transparent, open nakedness. Love is crazy—crazy enough to believe and crazy enough to love no matter what.

Love is blind; it is blind to every fault and negative behavior so it can see the best in us and inspire us to be our better self and show us the best in each other.

We all have love; we all have the ability to align with our polarity of attraction. We are different colors in the same mural, adding life and contrast that highlights each other. Men and women are not opposites; they are like two pieces of the same puzzle that interlock as one in sex and in life. When they come together to express their part of the portrait, greater beauty is shown. The feminine life energy flows around and through the man, causing him to be erect in life and to stand taller in every aspect and venue of life.

Men stand taller in more ways than one as the feminine energy fills our glasses. A free man, a man who stands in his power and is present in the moment, will embrace that energy and receive it with an open soul and then return it, which completes the flow of energy. It doesn't matter if it comes from a young lady or an elderly woman—or from being one with nature. He has the ability to allow the energy to breathe and move him and then return it with greater love.

When he is with his lover, he can call out the energy that he received and express it in the sex of love or share it with the touch of his finger as he brushes her cheek on their walk through the park. He can guide it with his heart and let it flow through his touch as kisses and intimate love. In freedom, he can only speak truth because love is free. He knows that lust is full of lies in its lowest level.

A man who stands in his power will never lie because lying is an act of giving away our power so we can look good in an attempt to please another. Honesty in the night is vital; without it, the heart commitment is shattered, the ability to guide the feminine is lost, and the feminine becomes the storm that rules the ship with no direction. If there is no honesty, there is no trust—and the sex of love becomes a cheap imitation of the Rolls-Royce or Bentley that it could have been.

With that, I include a poem that came to me one night. I questioned whether to include it or not, but I do it anyway to show what love is: open and honest in its transparency.

To feel you breathe as
Your breasts rise beneath me.
To feel the warmth of
Your body next to mine.
To experience your heart open as
I give my openness completely to you.
To become erect as
Your life energy flows around and through me.
Return and complete the flow
To give life.
Power flows through my fingers into you,

As I touch your angelic body.
Like silk to your cheeks and breasts,
Besos to your lips and skin.
Soft like eyelids, moist and warm,
In the silence the love grows strong.
Truth and honesty in the night,
There are no lies to whisper here.
In the heart commitment is
Bound to trust in all that is.
Back to you this energy flows,
Giving life as
I become one with you.

Love is crazy. Love is blind. Love is the wine and the song to fill the glass. Love is never-ending.